The Way Of
Faith

Seven Steps To Faith

DR. M. NATHANIEL ANDERSON PHD

PROISLE PUBLISHING

The contents of this work, including, but not limited to, the accuracy of events, people, and places depicted; opinions expressed; permission to used previously published materials included; and any advice given or actions advocated are solely the responsibility of the author, who assumes all liability for said work and indemnifies the publisher against any claims stemming from publication of the work.

All Rights Reserved

Copyright © 2022 by Dr. Michael Nathaniel Anderson. Ph.D.

No part of this book may be reproduced or transmitted in any form or by any means, electronic or mechanical, including photocopying, recording, or by any information storage and retrieval system, without permission in writing from the copyright owner. The views expressed in this work are solely those of the author and do not necessarily reflect the views of the publisher, and the publisher disclaims any responsibility for them.

Proisle Publishing Services LLC
1177 6th Ave 5th Floor
New York, NY 10036, USA
Phone: (+1 347-922-3779)
info@proislepublishing.com

ISBN: 978-1-959449-31-7

Table of Contents

1. Understanding Your Faith in Christ
2. Reading Every Day for Faith
3. Faith That Will Not Change
4. Believing and Confessing the Word
5. Establishing the Word of Faith
6. The Tongue, A Creative Force
7. You Will Process What You Speak
8. Scriptures to feed your faith

The Lord Jesus Christ said:

For it is the righteousness of Christ revealed from faith to faith; as it is written, The just shall live by faith. **Romans 1:17**

The Life Jesus came to give is the Faith Life

Through faith we understand that the worlds were framed by the word of God, so that things which are seen were not made of things which do appear. Hebrews 11:3

But without faith it is impossible to please Him: for He that comes to God must believe that He is, He is a rewarder of them that diligently seek Him. Hebrews 11:6

When you receive Jesus Christ as your Lord and Savior, you receive the gift of faith.

For by grace are we saved through faith; and that not of yourselves, it is the Gift of God. Ephesians 2:8

The faith life brings you into a personal relationship with God.

Behold, his soul which is lifted up is not up right in him: but the just shall live by faith. Habakkuk 2:4

The faith life means you will spend eternity in heaven in the very presence of the Lord Jesus Christ.

Whom, having not seen, ye love; in whom, through now ye see Him not, yet believing, ye rejoice with joy unspeakable and full glory!

Receiving the end of your faith, even the salvation of your souls. First Peter 1:8-9

The faith life is the present possession of every believer.

It is not something you must wait until after the death to receive you have faith life now!

Now faith is the substance of things hoped for, the evidence of things not seen. Hebrews 11:1

Now the just shall live by faith; but if any man draw back, my soul shall have no pleasure in him. Hebrews 10:38

Jesus also spoke about the ABUNDANT life. This refers to the life He wants you to experience in the here and now. The word abundant means bountiful, blessed, and joyful. The believer's life is meant to be radically different from your old life before Christ. The way of faith!

Therefore if any man be in Christ, he is a NEW creature: old things are passed away; behold, all things become NEW – Second Corinthians 5:17

That ye put off concerning the former conversation the old man, which is corrupt according to the deceitful lusts; and be renewed in the spirit of your mind; and that ye put on the NEW man, which after God is created in righteousness and true holiness. – Ephesians 4:22-24

Remember, As a Faith Believer, you have…

A New Nature – Second Peter 1:4

Whereby are given unto us exceeding great and precious promises: that by these ye might be partakers of the Divine Nature, having escaped the corruption that is in the world through lusts

A New Desire – Romans 10:17

Faith comes by hearing and hearing by the Word of God.

A New Love – Galatians 5:6

For in Jesus Christ neither circumcision availeth anything, nor uncircumcision, but faith which worketh by love.

New management – Second Peter 1:3

According as His divine power has given unto us all things that pertain unto life and godliness, through the knowledge of Him that has called us to glory and virtue;

A New Understanding – Galatians 2:20

I am crucified with Christ: nevertheless I live; yet not I, but Christ lives in me; and the life which I now live in the flesh I live by the faith of the Son of God, who loved me and gave himself for me.

This Bible workbook will present seven steps to living the faith life in Christ. These short lessons are designed to give you some basic truths concerning the believer's life as God intended for it to be. By looking up the Scriptures reference and answering the questions that will unlock the doors and open up the way of faith that leads to all the blessings of Heavenly Father has for you.

For verily I say unto you, Whosoever shall say unto this mountain, Be thou removed, and be thou cast into the sea; and shall not doubt in his heart, but shall believe that those things which he saith shall come to pass, he shall have whatever he saith. Therefore, I say unto you, whatever things ye desire, when he prays, believe that ye receive them, and he shall have them. Mark 11:23-24

CHAPTER ONE

Understanding Your Faith in Christ

The first step is to understand your standing or alignment in Christ. It is a glorious truth! Faith is fact and faith is an act!

Faith starts with Believing

1. God so loved the world that He gave His only begotten Son, that whoever - - - - - - in Him should not perish but have everlasting life – John: 3:16
2. Verily, verily, I say unto you, He that - - - - - - - - on me has everlasting life – John 6:47.
3. I come unto thee in a thick cloud, that the people may hear when I speak with thee, and - - - - - - thee forever – Exodus 19:9
4. But without faith it is impossible to please him; for he that cometh to God must - - - - - - that he is, and that he is a rewarder of them that diligently seek him – Hebrews 11:6
5. Therefore, I say unto you, whatever things ye desire, when ye pray, - - - - - that he received them, and he shall have them. – Mark 11:24
6. For with the heart man - - - - - - - - - unto righteousness; and with the mouth confession is made unto salvation – Romans 10:10
7. We, having the same spirit of faith, according as it is written, I - - - - - - -, and therefore have I spoken; we also - - - - - -, and therefore speak – Second Corinthians 4:13

Living the believer's life is not about you trying to look and acts like a believer. It is allowing the Lord Jesus Christ to live HIS life in and through you – sometime the Bible says is done by faith. Faith is simply believing God's Word and acting upon it.

What Is Faith And Where Does It Come from?

1. Now faith is the substance of - - - - - hoped for the evidence of - - - - - not seen – Hebrews 11:1
2. Simon Peter, a servant and an apostle of Jesus Christ, to them that have obtained like - - - - - - faith with us through the righteousness of God and our - - - - - -, Jesus Christ – Second Peter 1:1
3. Looking unto - - - - - -, the author and finisher of our faith, who for the joy that was set before - - - endured the cross, despising the - - - - -, and is set down – Hebrews at the right hand of the throne of - - - – Hebrews 12:2
4. And without faith it is impossible to please God, because - - - - -who comes to him must - - - - that he exists and that he rewards those who diligently seek him – Hebrews 11:6
5. Faith comes - - hearing and hearing by the - - - - - of God – Romans 10:17
6. And God - - -, let there be light: and there - - - light – Genesis 1:3. God released His - - - - - - in Words
7. And - - - - - - believed the Lord, and the Lord counted him as - - - - - - - - - - because of his faith – Genesis 15:6. NLT:

How Faith Is Built God's way.

1. Be doers of the word, and not - - - - - - only deceiving yours - - - selves – James 1:22
2. If ye abide in - - , and my words abide in you, ye shall ask what you - - - -, and it shall be done unto you – John 15:7
3. But ye, - - - - - - - - building up yourself on your most holy faith, - - - - - - - - - in the Holy Spirit – Jude 1:20
4. But without faith it is impossible to please - - -; for he that comes to God - - - - believe - - - - he is, and that he is a - - - - - - of them that diligently seek him. Hebrews 11:6
5. For by grace are ye saved through - - - - -; and that - - - of yourselves, it is the - - - - of God. Ephesians 2:8
6. We are bound to thank God always for you, brethren and as it is - - - - - - - -, because your - - - - - growth exceedingly, and the - - - - of every one of you all towards each other abounded. Second Thessalonians 1:3.
7. For in Christ Jesus - - - - - - - - circumcision availed anything, - - - uncircumcised, but faith - - - - - worked by love. Galatians 5:6
8. But what saith it? The - - - - is near the, even in thy - - - - -, and in thy heart; that is, the - - - - of faith, which we preach. Romans 10:8

Now, what does it mean to believe in Jesus? We all know that the word believe is a verb. We know that faith is a noun. Believing is a noun words; faith is the result of a person's having acted or believing. Believing in the New Testament sense, in the sense of the Paulina revelation, means possession action that ends with possession.

Notes:

CHAPTER TWO

Reading Every Day for faith

The Bible (the 1611 Authorized, King James Version) is your most important material possession. It is the Word of God!

The Bible Is a Supernatural Book

1. The Holy Scriptures were supernaturally given to us by - - - - - - - - - - of God – Second Timothy 3:6. This means the very Words of the Bible were breathed out of the mouth of God – Matthew 4:4.
2. The Scriptures were written down by Holy - - - of God as they were moved by the Holy - - - - - – Second Peter 1:21.
3. Every Word of God is - - - - – Proverbs 30:5. (Also: Psalms 12:6.)
4. The Words of God will never - - - - away – Matthew 24:35.
5. The LORD promised to provisionally - - - - His words for all generations – Psalms 12:7. (Also: Psalms 100:5.)

The Bible is my Authority in Faith

1. God cannot - - - – Titus 1:2.
2. The Word of God is - - - - - – John 17:17
3. The Word of God is forever - - - - - - - - – Psalms 119:89.
4. Whatsoever He said if unto you, - -, - - it was Mary's advice – John 2:5.
5. I must ask in faith – James 1:5, 6.
6. I must be a - - - - of the Word, not - - - - - - - only deceiving your own selves – James 1:22.

The Bible Is My Spiritual Food

1. The Bible is likened in to - - - - – First Peter 2:2.
2. The Bible is likened in to - - - - and - - - - - Hebrews 5:12-14.
3. The Bible is like into - - - - - - - – Matthew 4:4.
4. Job considered the - - - - of God to be more important than his - - - - - - - - food – Job 23: 12.

The Bible is My Guidebook for Faith

1. I am to walk by - - - - -, not by - - - - -- – Second Corinthians 5:7.
2. Faith comes by - - - -ing the Word of God – Romans 10:17.
3. I am to - - - - - - the Scriptures daily – John 9:39 and Acts 17:11.
4. The Bible is a lamp and a light for life's pathway – Psalms 119:105.
5. God will clean up my life as I take - - - - to (listen to and apply) His Word – Psalms 119:9
6. Memorizing God's Word will keep me from - - - - Psalms 119:11.
7. God has promised me - - - - success when I make - - - book my vital part of my life – Joshua 1:8.

If you have not already started, read through the Gospel according to John (the fourth book of the New Testament). After you have finished John's Gospel, read the First epistle of John (the 23RD book of the New Testament). So you will become more enlightened with Jesus as the pioneer of all faith.

You may know Him through the four Gospels, to a degree. You may know him more fully to the Pauline revelation. But you really get to know Him when you began to practice the Word.

Notes:

CHAPTER THREE

Faith That Will Not Change

The Word of God is incorruptible seed. A natural seed will sometimes fail: God's Word never fails. Many times people fail to apply the Word of God! True faith is a supernatural seed: it won't fail, but you can cause a failure in spite of the seed

Faith Is a Law

1. Therefore, we - - - - - - - - - that a man is justified by faith apart from the - - - - of the law – Romans 3:28
2. Because the carnal mind is enmity against God; for it is not subject to the - - - of God, neither, indeed, can be – Romans 8:7
3. Being born again, not of corruptible - - - -, but of incorruptible, - - the Word of God, then lived and abided forever – First Peter 1:23.
4. God forbid: yea, let God be true, but every man a liar; and it is - - - - - - -, That thou might be justified in thy sayings, and mightiest overcome when thou art judged – Romans 3:4
5. And the Lord said, if ye had faith as a grain of mustard seed, - - might - - - unto this sycamore tree, be the plucked up by the roots, and be thou planted in the sea; and it should obey you – Luke 17:6
6. Because the carnal mind is enmity against God; for it is not subject to the - - - of God, neither, indeed, can be – Romans 8:7
7. We, having the - - - - Spirit of faith, according as it is written, - believe, and therefore have - spoken; we also believe, and therefore speak – Second Corinthians 4:13.

8. For very I say unto you, whosoever's shall say unto this mountain, be thou removed, and be cast into the sea; and shall not doubt in his heart, but shall - - - - - - that those things which he - - - - it shall come to pass, he shall have whatever he - - - - – Mark 11:23

The Greatest Enemy of Faith

The only fight that the believer is call upon is the good fight of faith. And is there is a fight, then there must be enemies or hindrances to faith, there would be no fight to it.

1. My people are destroyed for lack of knowledge; because thou have rejected knowledge, I will also reject thee, that thou shall be no - - - - - - to me; seeing thou has forgotten the - - - of thy God, I will also forget thy children – Hosea 4:6.
2. Therefore if any - - - be in Christ, he is a new creature: old things are passed away; behold all things are become new – Second Corinthians 5:17.
3. For he has made Him to be - - - for us, who knew no - - -; that we might be made the righteousness of God in Him – Second Corinthians 5:21.
4. And he said unto them, why are you - - - - - - -, O ye of little faith? – Matthew 8:26
5. And immediately Jesus stretched forth His hand, and caught him, and said unto him O thou of little - - - - -, why didst thou - - - - - - ? – Matthew 14:31
6. Trust in the Lord with all thy heart, - - - lean not unto thine - - - understanding – Proverbs 3:5. (Human reasoning).

Love and Fear

1. For God has - - - given us a spirit of fear, but of power and of love and of a - - - - - -mind –**Second** Timothy 1:7
2. A son honors his father and a servant his master: if then I be a father, where is my honor? And if I be a master, where is my - - - -? – Malachi 1:6
3. The fear of the Lord is the beginning of wisdom – Psalms 111:10
4. Let us - - - - the conclusion of the whole matter; - - - - God, and keep His commandments; for this is the whole duty of man – Ecclesiastics 12:13
5. But - - - - - which worked by love – Galatians 5:6

Fear produces in-kind

1. The thing I are greatly feared has come upon me, and what I - - - - - - has happened to me – Job 3:25

2. Well, because of unbelief they were - - - - - - off, and thou - - - - -by faith. Be not high-minded, but fear – Romans 11: 20

3. For you have not received the spirit of bondage again to fear; but he have received the spirit of - - - - - - - - whereby we cry, Abba, Father – Romans 8:15

4. Neither gives - - - - - to the devil – Ephesians 4:27

Fear is no joke. It is a Bible fact. Fear produces its kind. It has power – power to torment and snare your soul; power to paralyze your potential, to render you ineffective, and to handicap you in life; power to produce in-kind. Remember that this fear is not a mental quirk but a action spirit that emanates from the enemy. Resist fear in Jesus name. Plead the blood of Jesus against every fear. Quote the words of God aloud against diabolical fear.

Notes:

_____
_____
_____
_____
_____
_____
_____
_____
_____
_____
_____
_____
_____
_____
_____
_____
_____
_____
_____
_____
_____
_____
_____
_____
_____
_____

CHAPTER FOUR

Believing and Confessing the Word

Whatever God says, He will perform. If you will notice throughout the Bible, God never did do anything that He did not say first. He said it, and then He did it. The power to do it was in the Word.

The Beginning Words

1. Through faith we understand that the worlds were framed by the word of God, so that - - - - - - which are seen were not made of - - - - - - which do appear – Hebrews 11:3
2. upholding - - things by the Word of - - - power – Hebrews 1:3
3. if you abide in - -, and my Words abide in you, you shall ask what you will and it shall be - - - - unto you – John 15:7
4. I believe, therefore have I - - - - - - -. I was greatly afflicted – Psalms 116:10
5. in the - - - - - - - - was the Word, and the Word was with God and the Word was God – John 1:1

The Word Made Flesh

1. And the Word - - - made flesh, and dwelt - - - - - us – John 1:14
2. In the beginning was the Word, and the Word was with God, and the - - - - was God – John 1:1
3. Be it unto me according to - - - Word – Luke 1:38

Only Believing

1. God so loved the world that He gave His only begot Son, that - - - - - - believes in Him shall not first but have everlasting life – John 3:16
2. He - - - believes in - - has everlasting life – John 6:37
3. And without faith it is impossible to please God, because anyone who comes to Him must - - - - - - that He exists and that He rewards those who earnestly seek Him – Hebrews 11:6
4. The time has come, he said. The kingdom of God has come near - - - - - - and believe the good news – Mark 1:15
5. Be not afraid, - - - - believe – Mark 5:36

Exercise the Spirit of Faith

1. out of abundance of the - - - - - the mouth speaks – Matthew 12:34
2. For bodily exercise - - - - - - little, but godliness is profitable unto all things, having promised of the life that now is, and of that which is to come – First Timothy 4:8
3. We, have the same - - - - - - of faith, according as it is written, I believe, and therefore have I spoken; we also believe, and therefore speak – Second Corinthians 4:13

Speak Success, Not Failure
1. So do not - - - -, for I am with you; do not be dismayed, for I am your- - -. I will strengthen you and help you; I will uphold you with my righteous right – Isaiah 41:10
2. Commit thy - - - - - unto the Lord, and thy thoughts shall be established – Proverbs 16:3

3. Then you will make your- - - prosperous, and then you will have - - - - success – Joshua 1:8
4. But - - - - - is the man who trust in the Lord, confidence is in Him – Jeremiah 17:7

It's not impossible for God to perform His every declaration. He can declare and do exactly what He says He going to do! And we find that God created man with the ability to operate in the same kind of faith. Control those words that come for out of your mouth and bring them into obedience to the word of God, which is God's spiritual law. In other words, that's where His power is, in the word, in what He says. Only believe.

Notes:

_____
_____
_____
_____
_____
_____
_____
_____
_____
_____
_____
_____
_____
_____
_____
_____
_____
_____

CHAPTER FIVE

Establishing the Word of Faith

Someone once told me, you have nothing, but Words. Words that win, if you will take Him as your Savior and Lord, victory will be yours again. He rejuvenates dead, worn- out hopes. He restores lost faith. He makes the voice vibrant again. He gives back loss health. He creates new opportunities. He gives the ability to have success. It's worth the chance – you have nothing to lose. You have all to gain. Words that win.

Walking by agreeing with Him

1. Can two - - - -together, unless they are agreed – Amos 3:3

2. And Enoch - - - - - - with God – Genesis 5:22

3. The Lord is - - helper; I will not - - - - what man shall do unto me.

4. For it is - - - - - - -, thou shall worship the Lord, thy God, and Him - - - - shall thou serve – Matthew 4:10

5. Nay, in all these things we are more than conquerors through Him that - - - - - us – Romans 8:37

6. Again I say to you, if two of you - - - - - on earth about anything that they may ask, it shall be done for them by my - - - - - - who is in heaven – Matthew 18:19

Faith Filled Words

1. No man - - - - fruit of thee hereafter forever. And His disciples heard it – Mark 11:14
2. Have faith - - God – Mark 11:22

3. Faith cometh by hearing, - - - hearing by the Word of God – Romans 10:17
4. He shall - - - - whatsoever - - saying – Mark 11:23
5. Let us hold - - - - to the profession of - - - faith – Hebrews 10:23
6. Before they - - - -, I will answer; and while they are still speaking, I will hear – Isaiah 65:24

Words That Work Wonders

1. I - - - -bless the Lord at all times; His praise shall continually be in my mouth – Psalms 34:1

2. They overcame him by the - - - - - of the lamb and by the Word of their testimony – Revelation 12:11

3. Let no corrupt Word proceed out of your - - - - -, but that which is good for necessary edification that it may - - - - - - grace to the hearers – Ephesians 4:29

4. Thou - - - snared with the Words of thy mouth; thou - - - taken with the Words of thy mouth – Proverbs 6:2

Become Word Conscious

1. A good man out of the - - - - treasure of his heart bring it forth good things; any evil man out of the - - - - treasure bring it forth evil things – Matthew 12:35
2. Whatever you ask the - - - - - - in my name, he will give it you – John 16:23
3. if ye abide in me and my words abide in you, you shall asked - - - - you will, and is shall be - - - - unto you – John 15:7
4. In this is my Father's glorified, that you - - - - - much fruit; so shall you be - - disciples – John 15:8.

5. If you - - - anything in - - name, I will do it. – John 14:14

Faith filled: We are faith filled when we are living life as God inspired us to live it, putting the Gospel into action through our deeds. Faith gives us believe and trust in God and in other people. We had to build on it every day through prayer, being part of the faith community and living out the gospel values

The Word of faith runs the Universe. True or false answers

God gave you the ability to use your tongue to create a better life by speaking words that are full of faith. The choice is yours, whether you will speak them or not.

1. Faith resides in the Spirit. True or false
2. Faith -filled words Sparks other 's faith. True or false
3. Faith works whether we agree or not. True or false
4. Faith is the fact and faith is the act. True or false
5. Start disagreeing with the word. True or false
6. God's word is natural law. True or false
7. Faith is a seed. True or false
8. Faith is the silence of authority. True or false
9. Words are without ability. True or false
10. Faith comes from man. True or false
11. God is a faith God. True or false

12. God releases His Faith in Words. True or false

13. What you already know about faith. True or false

Bold Bible Living. Yes or no answers

1. My constant appeal in the ministry is to live by God's word. Yes or no
2. Daring to act on the word of God, to do what God said we can do. Yes or no.
3. Confidence in Christ, not God, that enables us to shout. Yes or no
4. Fear, the ability of God that enables us to live free from fear all our days. Yes or no
5. I will not fail you. Yes or no
6. You, too, can be guided by God. You can hear his voice. Yes or no
7. Fear has one source – the devil.
8. Yes or no
9. God has given us the spirit of power.
Yes or no

10. We won't be prideful for love is puffed up.

Yes or no

11. He operated in the God kind of faith. Yes or no

The supernatural realm of faith: Fill in the blank

1. The new birth is a _____.
2. Faith the _____ birth
3. He operated in the God _____ of faith.
4. Faith-filled Words release out of your _____.
5. Faith filled _____ Will Put You over.
6. Fear-filled Words Will Defeat _____.
7. _____ are the most powerful thing in the universe
8. Faith will make prayer _____.
9. Prayer Won't Work _____ faith.

10. It Was God honoring _____ filled words.

The Words You Speak Will either put you over in life will hold you in bondage. Many people have been held captive in their circumstances by their own words. The absence of God's word in your life will rob you of your faith in His ability. Learn to speak His faith- filled words to your situation and see your life transformed. Allow God's creative power to flow from you.

Notes:

_____
_____
_____
_____
_____
_____
_____
_____
_____
_____
_____
_____
_____
_____
_____
_____
_____
_____
_____
_____
_____
_____

CHAPTER SIX

The tongue, a Creative Force

Put yourself in position to receive God's best for you by speaking His Word. God's creative power is still just as it was in the beginning of time, when He stood and said, Light – be, and light was. His Word spoke from your mouth and conceived in your heart becomes a spiritual force releasing His ability within you. Come see the power show up in you!

Watch Your Words

1. Forever O' Lord, thy Word is - - - - - - in heaven – Psalms 119:89
2. The mouth of the righteous man is a - - - of life – Proverbs 10:11
3. The mouth of the - - - - bring it forth wisdom – Proverbs 10:31
4. The - - - - of the righteous know if what is acceptable – Proverbs 10:31
5. Put - - - - from thee a crooked - - - - -, a perverse lips from thee – Proverbs 4:24

Authority of Words

1. For by the words thou shall be justified, and by thy words thou shall be condemned God's word as authority Scripture
2. When the king heard the words of the book of the law, he - - - - his clothes – Second Kings 22:11
3. The Grass Witted, the Flowers fades, but the word of our God - - - - - - for ever
4. Giving You Power to Tread over Serpents and Scorpions, and over all the - - - - - - of the enemy;

and nothing shall by any means hurt you – Luke 10:19

Words Are Your Ability
1. You are God's, - - - - - - children, and have overcome them, because greater is He that is in you, then he that is in the world – First John 4:4
2. A man has joy by the answer of his mouth; and a word spoken in due season, how good is it! – Proverbs 15:23
3. The heart of a wise teach of his mouth, and add of learning to his lips – Proverbs 16:23
4. The Words of a man's mouth are like deep waters, and the wellspring of wisdom like a flowing brook – Proverbs 18:4

Spirit Words
1. The words that I - - - - - - unto you they are spirit and they are life – John 6:63
2. Create in me a clean heart, O God, and - - - - - a steadfast spirit within me – Psalms 51:10
3. I will put my Spirit - - - - - - - you and cause you to walk in My statutes, and you will keep My judgment and do them – Ezekiel 36:27
4. God is spirit, and - - - - - who worship Him must worship Him in spirit and truth – John 4:24

Faith for Giving
1. And whatever we ask, we received from Him, because we - - - - His commandments, and do those things that are pleasing in - - - sight – First John 3:22

2. Give and it will be given to - - -; good measure, pressed - - - -, shaken together and running over. – Luke 6:38
3. My - - - run of over. – Psalms 23:5
4. Freely you - - - - - - - - -, freely give. – Matthew 10:8.

God created the universe by the method which we have just put into motion by the words of your mouth. God released his faith in words. If the body of Christ would grasp the truth and the principles that are taught in this book and put them in action, they would change their world overnight! Jesus said I have told my people they can have what they say, but my people are saying what they have. Words are the most powerful things in the universe.

Notes:

CHAPTER SEVEN

You Will Possess What You Speak

Your speaking of faith precedes your possession of what you are desiring and seeking. You can walk with God daily by agreeing with Him and His Word. Because He had said it, we may boldly say it, too if we speak only that our senses dictate, we will not be agreeing with God.

1. Speak Jesus as Lord (Romans 10:8-9), and you will possess salvation.
2. Speak that by His stripes we are healed (Isaiah 53:5), and you will possess healing.
3. Speak that the love of God has been poured out in your heart by the Holy Spirit (Romans 5:5), and you will possess the ability to love everyone.
4. Speak that the righteousness are bold as a lion (Proverbs 28:1), and you will possess lionhearted boldness in spiritual warfare.
5. Speak that God will never leave you nor forsake you (Hebrews 13:5), and you will possess the presence of God by each step you take.
6. Speak that you are the redeemed of the Lord (Psalms 107:2), and you will possess redemption benefits every day.
7. Speak that the anointing which you had received from God abides in you (First John 2:27), and your yokes will be destroyed because of the anointing (Isaiah 10:27).
8. Speak that in the name of Jesus you can cast out demons (Mark 16:17), and you will possess dynamic deliverance over Satan's power.

9. Speak that they will lay hands on the sick, and they will recover (Mark 16:18), and you will possess healing for the oppressed.
10. Speak that you are a branch of the living Vine (John 15:5), and you possess Vine life where ever you go.

11. Speak that you are the temple of the living God (Second Corinthians 6:16), and you will possess the reality of God dwelling in you and walking in you.
12. Speak that God shall supply all you need according to His riches in glory by Christ Jesus (Philippians 4:19), and you will possess God supply for your every need.

How can we walk with God in power, blessings, and usefulness? By agreeing with God that we have: what He says we have: His Name, His nature, His power, His authority, and His love. We agreed that we have what God says in His Word that we have. We cannot truly walk with God unless we agree with Him through Jesus faith.

Notes:

_____
_____
_____
_____
_____
_____
_____
_____

CHAPTER EIGHT

Memorizing Scriptures to feed faith

Scripture memorization is hiding God's word in your heart. The Bible says: thy words have I hid in my heart that I might not sin against the (Psalms 119:11). When you memorize portions of the Bible you'll be amazed how the Holy Spirit will bring them to mind at certain times and in various situations.

The key to memorization is repetition. Read a Scripture portion out loud several times during the day and it won't be long before it's in your heart. Review it frequently to keep it there.

Beginning by memorizing ONE, verse – then add another, then another, and so on. Don't forget to include the address (chapter and verse) in the memorization.

Here are some key verses to begin memorizing:

I. I am to live my new life by the faith of the Son of God. – Galatians 2:20

ii. The just (saved) are to live by faith. – Romans 1: 17

iii. Memorizing the Word will keep you from sin. Psalms 119:11

IV. Jesus said unto him, if thou can believe, all things are possible to him that believes it. – Mark 9:23

V. Without faith it Is Impossible to please God. – Hebrews 11:6.

VI. Therefore, being justified by faith, we have peace with God through our Lord Jesus Christ. – Romans 5:1.

VII. So then faith comes by hearing and hearing by the word of God. – Romans 10:17.

VIII. Give, and it shall be given unto you; good measure, pressed down, and shaken together, and running over, shall men give into your bosom. For with the same measure that you give withal it shall be measured to you again. – Luke 6:38

Notes:

_____
_____
_____
_____
_____
_____
_____
_____
_____
_____
_____
_____
_____
_____
_____
_____
_____
_____
_____
_____

www.ingramcontent.com/pod-product-compliance
Lightning Source LLC
LaVergne TN
LVHW021050100526
838202LV00082B/5428